P9-DFA-787

P9-DFA-787

# LAUREL & HARDY

# LAUREL & HARDY

## Annie McGarry

CHARTWELL
BOOKS, INC.

28173141

Published by
**CHARTWELL BOOKS, INC.**
A Division of **BOOK SALES, INC.**
110 Enterprise Avenue
Secaucus, New Jersey 07094

Produced by
Brompton Books Corp.
15 Sherwood Place
Greenwich, CT 06830

Copyright © 1992 Brompton Books Corp.

ISBN 1-55521-792-3

Printed in Hong Kong

Designed by Ruth DeJauregui

**Page 1:** *Their real-life roles were reversed in their film personae. Stan Laurel was the dominant one in their partnership, while Ollie dominated Stanley in the films. This still illustrates another inversion of real life—Oliver, an inveterate card player, would never have lost a game to Stan.*

**Page 2-3:** *Had they never become partners, Stan and Oliver's careers would have been considered moderately successful. Once established as a team, however, their popularity skyrocketed.*

**Right:** *Ollie seems to be chastising Stanley for another fine mess in this Hal Roach Studios publicity still.*

# CONTENTS

# STAN & OLIVER

### Stan

From the moment Arthur Stanley Jefferson came into the world on 16 June 1890, he seemed born to be a comedian. His mother, Madge Metcalfe, was a vaudeville actress, and in the space marked 'Occupation' on little Stan's birth certificate, his father, Arthur J Jefferson, designated himself 'Comedian' — a fact which was to greatly please his son.

From his earliest childhood in Ulverston, England, Stan asked his father, who had developed into a vaudevillian writer, producer, performer and theatre owner, for toys that had to do with entertainment: puppets, costumes and miniature theatres. He spent hours mimicking the comics he saw every night on his father's stage. As a boy, he wrote and produced plays on a stage in his basement, until the fateful performance during which he literally set the stage on fire, permanently closing the venue.

Away at some of England's best schools but not a good student, Stan fortunately was encouraged to be a clown, even giving private command performances for some of the teachers during study hours. He later wished that he had studied more, because he thought that more schooling might have made him funnier.

He made his debut at age 16 under his real name — Stan Jefferson — at a tiny museum-cum-theatre. Soon he was touring Europe and America with Fred Karno's London Comedians, often playing understudy to his roommate, Charlie Chaplin. When Chaplin left to join Mack Sennet's Keystone Film Company in 1913, the troupe abruptly disbanded. For awhile, Stan supported himself by doing his impression of Chaplin's Little Tramp for crowds who were hungry for the sight of the newest star.

From 1914 to 1922, Stan toured American vaudeville houses with a number of different partners, including Baldwin Cooke, who would later be a familiar face in Laurel & Hardy shorts. Mae Charlotte Dahlberg Cuthbert became his partner off-stage as well as on, in a stormy common-law marriage that lasted until 1925. When Stan became concerned that there might be a bad omen in his name because it contained 13 letters, it was Mae who rechristened him. She had found his new stage name in an illustration of a Roman general wearing a wreath of laurel.

Welcoming the stability of film work after constant traveling, Stan settled in California and appeared in his first film, **Nuts in May**, at the

**Previous page:** *These pilgrims, shown here in a Hal Roach promotional photo, never seem to make too much progress.*

**Right:** *Stan with his wife Lois Neilson Laurel and their only daughter, Lois, who was born in 1927.*

**Opposite:** *'Professor Padilla expected to startle the medical world with his new theory—that the human brain has a level surface—in some instances, practically flat.'—the opening title of* Habeas Corpus *(1928). Stanley certainly seems to fit the description in this publicity still.*

age of 27. He signed his first long-term contract with Hal Roach in 1926. He had yet to develop the character which would bring him fame and immortality. In the 60 or more films he made before teaming with Oliver Hardy, he played by turns a brash go-getter or a dimwitted stooge.

## Oliver

Norvell Hardy was born in Harlem, Georgia on 18 January 1892. His father, Oliver, who was a popular lawyer and local politician, died when Norvell was young, and the boy took his name to honor his memory. The family soon moved to nearby Madison, where Mrs Hardy began running a hotel. Young Oliver spent hours in the lobby, indulging in what was to be a lifelong habit—people watching. He developed much of his comedy from the observations he made of people's gestures, attitudes and behavior. When people asked him how he possibly invented such an outrageous character, Oliver always responded that the world was populated by thousands of people just like Ollie.

At the age of eight, Oliver was given permission to join a troupe of entertainers, Coburn's Minstrels. After a few weeks of touring as a boy soprano, homesickness drove Oliver back to Madison. Music continued to preoccupy him, and he convinced his mother to send him to study voice in Atlanta. When his mother arrived for a visit, she discovered that he hadn't attended classes for weeks, but was singing in front of slides for 50 cents a day. His mother promptly sent him off to military school, where he remained until he was 18.

Just after graduation, Hardy opened the first movie theatre in Milledgeville, Georgia and became interested in acting. He decided that he couldn't be any worse an actor than the ones he saw in the films, so he headed to Jacksonville, Florida, then a burgeoning movie-making capital, to become an actor.

From 1914 to 1917, Hardy worked for a number of small studios and appeared in over 100 comedies, playing mostly comic villains. He joked later, 'My weight just automatically made me a heavy.' He and the other young actors would go to an Italian barber for their daily

MGMP. 7945

MGMP·16674

**Above: *Stan Laurel and Oliver Hardy were known for more than their film-making talents on the Lot of Fun. Oliver had a beautiful singing voice, and Stan, like any good vaudevillian, could pick up most instruments and start to play. While working on a film, Stan and Oliver would occasionally wander off to a deserted soundstage and begin to harmonize. Stagehands, actors, writers—everyone would come from all over the studio to listen or join in on these impromptu concerts.***

**Here they join 'The Happy-Go-Lucky Trio'—Vern Trimble on banjo, Art Stephenson on sax, and the composer of 'The Dance of the Cuckoo' and other Laurel & Hardy soundtrack classics, T Marvin Hatley, is on the stand-up bass and cornet. In typical Lot of Fun fashion, they dressed for the occasion.**

shaves. This barber finished Hardy's shave by rubbing his chubby cheeks with talcum powder and cooing, 'Nice-a babee!' Hardy soon had the nickname 'Baby,' later shortened to 'Babe,' which became his lifelong sobriquet. He was even billed as Babe Hardy in a few early movies, until a numerologist told him that he would find success under the name Oliver Hardy.

In 1918, Hardy moved to California and worked for a number of different studios there, including Hal Roach Studios, where he met director Leo McCarey. By 1926, Hardy was under long-term contract to Roach.

## Then There Were Two

In 1919, nothing seemed auspicious about the new film **The Lucky Dog**. Two young comedians, both under contract to Hal Roach, were bound to work on the same films eventually, and **The Lucky Dog** marked the first Laurel and Hardy appearance in a film together. Stan played a young vagrant who makes friends with a stray dog, and Oliver played a robber who bumps into the young man and accidentally puts the loot into his pocket. Though the dialogue was far different than anything in their Laurel & Hardy comedies, there is one scene in which aspects of their future partnership is foreshadowed. Ollie tells Stanley—via title—to 'Put 'em both up, insect, before I comb your hair with lead.' Stan puts his hands in the air, and turns a complete circle,

coming around to face an exasperated Ollie with an expression of complete incomprehension.

It was another seven years before Stan and Oliver acted together in a film, although Stan did direct Oliver in several at the Roach Studios. Oliver continued to play comic villains.

In 1925, Oliver played an inept paperhanger who, in retrospect, seems like a prototype for the familiar Ollie of the Laurel & Hardy films. The derby hat, the toothbrush mustache, the flowery gestures and the disgusted 'takes' into the camera are all there.

**Above: 'Neither Mr Laurel nor Mr Hardy had any thoughts of doing wrong. As a matter of fact, they had no thoughts of any kind.' The opening title from The Hoosegow (1929) seems just as appropriate for this publicity photo from their later movie, The Big Noise (1944).**

# THE LOT OF FUN

In 1926, Stan began working for Hal Roach Studios as a director and writer, and occasionally filled in when another actor was needed. He was so pleased with these behind-the-scene tasks that he didn't miss full-time performing. Oliver Hardy, working there as one of the Comedy All-Stars, Roach's stable of comedians, was appearing as the butler in **Get 'Em Young** (1926), a film directed by Stan. Oliver scalded himself while cooking one night, and the studio asked Stan to fill Oliver's role. A reluctant Stan, who enjoyed working behind the camera, was persuaded to perform only by an increase in salary. By the following year, 1927, Stan and his new partner had become so successful that Stan had to reconcile himself to the idea of being a comedian again.

Director Leo McCarey saw the potential for Stan and Oliver to be ideal partners, not just because of their comically contrasting figures, but 'also because they seemed to have this solid instinct that only top-flight comedians have of the *reality* underlying a gag. They were both great actors, and could have played serious stuff quite easily.'

McCarey encouraged the writers to create bigger and bigger roles for the two of them, while diminishing the roles of the other comics. Gradually, Stan and Oliver evolved into a comedy duo.

Both Stan and Oliver appeared in **Forty-Five Minutes From Hollywood** (1926), but they don't exchange as much as a hello. They first played as a team in **Duck Soup** (1927), which Stan based on a vaudeville sketch written by his father, Arthur J Jefferson. Stan wrote himself in as one of the hobos on the run, as per Hal Roach's instructions to write parts for himself in more scripts. The other hobo is cast in the original script as Syd Crossley, but somehow, Oliver Hardy ended up with the part. Despite the fact that several people on the lot — including their future director, Leo McCarey — remarked upon the incredible chemistry between the two actors, they continued to make movies separate from one another.

In **Slipping Wives** (1927), Stan and Oliver appeared in the same film, but the team feeling of **Duck Soup** was gone. Their characters were 'bitter enemies,' in the words of the script.

Oliver had bit parts in the next couple of Laurel's films: **Love 'Em and Weep** (1927) and **Why Girls Love Sailors** (1927). In **With Love and Hisses** (1927), they were pitted against each other again. In **Sailors, Beware!** (1927), the Boys were given more scenes together, and people around the studio began to refer to them as 'Laurel & Hardy.' They were very slowly becoming a team, as they individually honed the characters that would become Stanley and Ollie.

14

**Previous page: *Fay Holderness is giving futile instructions in a classic Laurel & Hardy predicament from* Hog Wild *(1930).***

Then, in May 1927, **Do Detectives Think?** was written and filmed. It was the first film since **Duck Soup** that had allowed Laurel and Hardy to act as a team. This film marks the debut of the rumpled-but-dignified suits, which were to become their sartorial tradition. Because they were cast as detectives, they wore derbies, thereby introducing what was to become their emblem.

Three films later, they made **The Second Hundred Years** (1927), because someone at Roach Studios finally demanded that they be yoked together as partners. Leo McCarey, a free-spirited Irishman, had been a lawyer, a miner and a songwriter before trying his hand at comedy writing. After writing for the **Our Gang** series, he worked his way up to being a respected director.

Anxious to get back to directing and writing, Stan resisted McCarey's suggestion. Oliver Hardy was much more amenable. He was looking for a partner and a steady position as a featured player. It was not exactly an auspicious beginning for one of Hollywood's greatest comedy teams. Against Stan's wishes, the two comedians became a team.

About half of the early press releases refer to the comedy team as Hardy and Laurel, and some call them a 'famous comedy trio,' implying James Finlayson as the third. Hal Roach began to actively promote the two of them as a team, and history was in the making. By the end of 1927, the team was so popular that they hardly needed the publicity.

Around the time of the making of **Pardon Us** (1931), the relationship between Hal Roach and Stan Laurel began to fall apart. Roach began to tighten down on the Lot of Fun — as the Roach Studio lots were known in their heyday — trying to wring higher profits out of his studio. In the early days, the quality of the films and the happiness of his employees had been his highest priorities, but as he began to feel the economic pressure of the Great Depression, he began to demand feature-length films from Laurel & Hardy. **Pardon Us** was originally intended to be a two-reeler, but Roach decided to make the film a feature despite Stan's protests.

Roach also became concerned about the adverse publicity about Stan's — and, to a lesser extent, Oliver's — peccadillos. He worried that Stan didn't have the wholesome reputation necessary to a family entertainer. He made Stan sign a legal document promising that he would not do anything to bring public disapproval upon himself. It's not inconceivable that Roach also was aware of Stan's prodigious talent and the respect he received around the studio, and that Roach was jealous of Stan.

Stan was a victim of his own success. Laurel & Hardy brought so much prosperity to the studio that Roach could now spend more money on each film, thereby enhancing his own reputation as a feature film producer, but Stan's creative control dwindled as the budget and Hal's power increased.

Roach began to constrict Stan's power on the set. Stan had always been the de facto director and writer of his movies, with a director there to take care of the details. Most of them had the sense to know that Stan was a comic genius comparable to Charlie Chaplin, and that it was best for everyone simply to cooperate with him. Roach, however, felt it necessary to interfere, and forced the team to play comic relief in feature-length productions such as **The Devil's Brother** (1933) and other disastrous films. Though Stan tried to reach an agreement with Roach, Roach terminated his contract.

Roach then tried to worry Stan and curry Hardy's favor by giving him the chance to have his own series, but Hardy turned it down. The show

of solidarity with Stan forced Roach to negotiate another contract with Stan. In December of 1938, however, Roach filed a deposition with the courts stating that Stan caused problems through a 'refusal to accept instructions.' He elaborated, saying that Stan didn't cooperate with the other people who were working on the pictures, that he often changed the ideas of the scripts and that he wasn't giving his full attention to the film. Roach wanted a tame Stan who would obediently and reliably turn out money-making movies, inspired or not.

Stan needed to feel that he could impose his vision on his work, not because he was a megalomaniac, but because the final result was so important to him. Unfortunately, during the making of **Swiss Miss** (1938), a time when Stan most needed to prove himself as a filmmaker, he experienced another personal upheaval. He divorced his second wife and married his third the next day. His second wife then chased him down during his honeymoon, claiming that they had never divorced and that Stan was a bigamist. He duly produced his divorce papers and obtained a restraining order against her, but Roach, who was spending a lot of money on the film, was a nervous wreck about the state of Stan's affairs.

Towards the end of the making of **Blockheads** in 1938, Stan disappeared without a word, possibly in reaction to some news about the picture he had just completed. The classic scene in **Swiss Miss**, in which Stan and Ollie carry a piano across a bridge, had been rendered almost unintelligible by an unnecessary re-editing job which Roach had performed without Stan's consent.

Two days after his defection, Stan wired Roach a telegram wondering where his paycheck was and stating that he was ready to go back to work. Roach, however, was unnerved by Stan's unexplained disappearance. The studio treasurer gave Stan's secretary his final paycheck and told him that Stan was off the Roach payroll as of 12 July 1938.

Roach hired comedian Harry Langdon, signing him to do a series of films with Hardy. **Zenobia** (1939) was the only one that was ever made, because when Oliver's contract came up for renewal with Roach, he refused to sign. Instead, he and his partner went to Twentieth Century-Fox and, through their attorney and old friend, Ben Shipman, Laurel and Hardy signed a contract.

MGMP-13652

**Above: *Stanley and Ollie getting fleeced by 'Farina' of Our Gang fame in* Forty-Five Minutes from Hollywood.**

## Forty-Five Minutes From Hollywood (1926)

Stanley and Ollie share a derby and their cash with 'Farina' (Allen Clayton Hoskins), one of the early stars from Hal Roach's **Our Gang** series. In the actual film, however, they don't even exchange a hello. ***Forty-Five Minutes from Hollywood*** featured a number of Hal Roach's stars, including the **Our Gang** kids.

## Do Detectives Think? (1927)

Laurel plays Ferdinand Finkleberry, 'the second worst detective in the whole world,' and Hardy is Sherlock Pinkham — 'the worst.' The opening title reads, 'This story opens with a lot of people in court — most of them should be in jail.' The Boys are hired to guard Judge Foozle (played by James Finlayson) from an escaped murderer, The Slasher, whom the judge sentenced to death. The Slasher has escaped and, seeking revenge, is masquerading as the judge's butler.

The Boys wore their infamous derby hats for the first time in this early film, and performed the routine in which Stanley hands Ollie the wrong hat, then hands Ollie the wrong hat, then hands Ollie the wrong hat, then, finally, hands Ollie the wrong hat. At the end of the film, Stanley hands Ollie the wrong hat.

**Above:** *The Boys finally realize the butler really is the escaped murderer in* **Do Detectives Think?**

**Left:** *Laurel and Hardy have broken out of prison in* **The Second Hundred Years.**

## The Second Hundred Years (1927)

Convicts Stanley and Ollie's attempted jailbreak lands them right in the warden's office. An instant box office smash, this film's ratings went right through the ceiling. Having established Laurel & Hardy as household names, the studio decided to immediately begin filming their next film, **Call of the Cuckoos** (1927), without waiting for the Boys' hair to grow out.

**Above and opposite: *Laughing uncontrollably, Laurel and Hardy wait for their ticket from Edgar Kennedy in* Leave 'Em Laughing.**

## Leave 'Em Laughing (1928)

Stanley has a toothache, and after Ollie fails to pull it out in the traditional manner—tying the tooth to a door and slamming it—he takes Stanley to the dentist. Ollie tries to quiet Stan's fears by sitting in the dentist's chair himself, but the distracted dentist gives Ollie some laughing gas and goes to work before Ollie can protest.

When Ollie becomes conscious, he throws Stanley down in the chair and gives him some laughing gas. By the time they get out to the car, the nitrous oxide has them roaring with laughter—especially when they crash into a taxi and cause a traffic jam. When policeman Edgar Kennedy threatens to take them to jail, they only howl louder.

## The Finishing Touch (1928)

Stanley and Ollie go to work as professional house finishers, much to the chagrin of nurse Dorothy Coburn who, in protest of the noise, punches Stanley and Ollie. Ollie, ever the gentleman, restrains an incensed Stan from punching her back, but in the end the quarrelsome nurse—Miss Coburn's stand-up—lands in the wet cement.

## You're Darn Tootin' (1928)
## (British title: The Music Blasters)

The opening title reads, 'The story of two musicians who played neither by note nor ear—they used brute strength.' A title tells us, 'The orchestra leader was making his farewell appearance—the public had been demanding it for years.'

Out of synch with the rest of the orchestra but in perfect harmony with each other, Stanley and Ollie are nevertheless fired, and Stanley weeps some of his famous tears.

Out of work and down on their luck, the two fellows battle one another. Ollie breaks Stan's clarinet, and Stanley throws Ollie's horn into the street where a truck squashes it flat. Drawn into the scuffle, each passerby vengefully pulls off the pants of another until a policeman (Christian Frank) arrives to find Stanley and Ollie in a pile of pants and, of course, another fine mess.

**Above: Archetypical sailors on leave, the Boys are trying to pick up girls in Two Tars.**

**Right: After getting stuck in a traffic jam, the Two Tars cut loose—on Baldwin Cooke's car!**

### *Two Tars* (1928)

Sailors Laurel and Hardy introduce themselves to the lovely ladies as Ensign Laurel and Secretary Wilbur—the Secretary of the Navy in 1928—and go for a pleasant Sunday drive in the countryside, which of course turns disastrous, ending with the famous 'train in the tunnel' scene.

*Two Tars* was the first of 30 films with Laurel & Hardy for both Baldwin Cooke, who played the countryside motorist in this film, and Harry Bernard, who played the truck driver.

## *Liberty* (1929)

In the process of escaping from prison, convicts Stanley and Laurel have switched pants. They spend the rest of the two reels trying to switch them back. The premise of the movie was taken from a scene cut out of **We Faw Down** (1928), the film they had made just before this one. **We Faw Down** was too long, and the very funny pants-trading scenes were the only expendable ones.

When this film was made, rear screen projection was still in the experimental stages, so the crew built a three-story structure of wood made to look like steel. Director Leo McCarey and Hal Roach's biggest stars were working almost 200 feet above the ground with a wooden platform as a safety measure.

At one point in the 12 day shoot, Laurel looked down and began to panic. To calm him down by proving how safe they were, Hardy jumped down to the wooden platform. Being made of sugar pine, the platform promptly broke. Fortunately for Oliver, a member of the construction crew, Thomas Benton Roberts, after complaining to no avail about using such soft wood, had taken it upon himself to set up a safety net under the platform. Hardy's fall was thereby 20 feet instead of 200, and he quickly resumed shooting, only slightly bruised and shaken.

At top: *High up on a skyscraper, the Boys dangle over the city in* Liberty. *Happily, all ends well* (above).

**Above:** *Poor Edgar Kennedy has a sore foot and would rather stay home but Laurel and Hardy and their wives convince him it's A Perfect Day for a picnic.*

## A Perfect Day (1929)

This film was distinguished by its pioneering in the field of sound effects and marks the first appearance of Hardy's plaint, 'Why don't you do something to help me?' As a parson passes the picnickers on the street, Edgar Kennedy, as the gouty Uncle Edgar, mutters 'Oh, s—-!,' a line that surely was not in the script.

## Wrong Again (1929)

Quiet on the set. Stable hands Stanley and Ollie are busily caring for the prize horse, Blue Boy, when they overhear two men discussing the latest news: the famous *Blue Boy* has been stolen, and there is a $5,000 reward for its return. Meanwhile, the *Blue Boy* they are discussing—Thomas Gainsborough's famous painting—has been recovered by the police, who have contacted the owner by telephone. The owner instructs them to bring it right over.

Stanley and Ollie head over to the house. When the owner of the painting raises a window, Ollie calls out, 'We've brought your Blue Boy.'

The owner throws down his keys, replying, 'Take him right into the house.' Bewildered, the Boys comply with his wishes.

'These millionaires are so peculiar,' says Ollie in an aside to Stanley. 'Even now he's taking a bath, and its only Monday.'

The man calls down from a balcony, 'Put him on the piano, would you mind?'

Stanley succeeds in luring the horse up onto the beautiful grand piano in the elegant mansion, but when Stanley jumps down, so does Blue Boy. After several hilarious attempts to get the horse up on the piano again, Ollie and Stanley finally accomplish their task, dislodging a piano leg in the process. Ollie must then support the weight of the horse on the grand piano.

When the two-dimensional *Blue Boy* arrives, it is destroyed in the fray resulting from the discovery of the other Blue Boy. Stanley and Ollie are chased off by the shotgun-toting owner, who shoots the policeman by mistake.

**Above: *The Boys and Blue Boy, the horse, are patiently waiting for the next take on the set of Wrong Again.***

**Right:** *In Berth Marks Laurel and Hardy are itinerant musicians who have nearly missed their station, but where are their instruments?*

**Opposite, above:** *Jean Harlow is courting disaster with Laurel and Hardy working as the doormen in Double Whoopee.*

**Opposite, below:** *With the rest of her dress still caught in the car door, Jean Harlow signs into the hotel while the Boys and desk clerk, Rolfe Sedan, look on in shock.*

## Berth Marks (1929)

In their second talking film, Stanley and Ollie play vaudevillians who must travel by train to Pottsville overnight to do a show. Their first 'talkie,' aptly titled *Unaccustomed As We Are* (1929), had been made on a sound stage, but this film was shot on location in a train yard, crowded with curious Laurel & Hardy fans. The director, Lewis R Foster, concerned himself with editing out the sound of their giggling, until eventually Stan and Ollie succumbed to giggling themselves, and had to go play golf together until their heads cleared. The scene in which Ollie and Stanley must sleep together in a narrow upper berth took three days to film because the Boys had to keep pausing to regain their straight faces. The dialogue was almost entirely improvised.

## Double Whoopee (1929)

Billed as Harlean McGrew II, a 19-year-old Jean Harlow made her first film appearance as a glamorous woman who loses the entire back of her dress in the door of a taxi which doorman Stanley has slammed.

Instead of accruing the additional expense of giving Harlow her own screen test, the Hal Roach Studios simply cast Harlow in this film to see how she appeared on film. Later, MGM wooed Harlow away from the stories with the promise of more money, as they would later recruit Laurel & Hardy with promises of giving them more creative control than Hal Roach. Before she left she made *The Bacon Grabbers* (1929), and after her move to Metro, she lent herself—in a photograph only—to Hal Roach to appear as Jeanie-Weenie, Ollie's lost amour and the sweetheart of the Foreign Legion, in the 1931 film *Beau Hunks* (1931).

On the first take, neophyte actress Harlow approached the hotel lobby desk in a transparent slip. Character actor Rolfe Sedan, who played the desk clerk, recalled: 'It was a shock for all of us. When she came up to the desk, for a moment I almost didn't say my lines. Even though I'd been in burlesque, they didn't walk around like that.' For the second take, Harlow was outfitted with a less revealing slip.

**Above: *Ollie gets both girls while Stanley sobs in* Men O' War.**

**Right: *The Boys mug for the camera in* Men O' War.**

## *Men o' War* (1929)

Ollie and Stanley have gone out to enjoy a day in the park, but the situation becomes complicated when they begin to compete with each other for the attention of two charming women, played by Gloria Greer and Anne Cornwall.

## Big Business (1929)

Stanley and Ollie go into business for themselves, selling Christmas trees door-to-door in July. At the first two houses, the Boys suffer rejection and a blow with a hammer over Ollie's head. At the third house, James Finlayson's refusal of their offer only makes the Boys more determined to sell him a tree. Their perseverance infuriates Fin (as he was known on the set), and he hacks up the sample tree with a big pair of shears.

This affront sets Stanley and Ollie on a spree of destruction. While Fin rips up the rest of the trees in the back of Stanley and Ollie's car, Stanley attacks Fin's house with an ax. Then Fin begins to destroy their car.

The house used in the film belonged to an employee of Hal Roach Studios. He was well compensated for the demolition of his home.

**Above: *Although Christmas trees really are Big Business, they don't sell too well in July, especially when Laurel and Hardy are involved. A frustrated James Finlayson takes an ax to both the trees and the car.***

**Above:** *Laurel and Hardy perform card tricks in* **Hollywood Review of 1929.**

**Opposite:** *Stanley gets a sharp surprise from Ollie in* **Rogue Song.**

## Hollywood Revue of 1929 (1929)

Once the studios had converted to sound, they were anxious to showcase the singing and dancing talents of their stars, even if their stars were severely lacking in these abilities. One of the many 'revues' to flaunt its 'All Singing, All Talking, All Dancing' medium, this film has the dubious attribute of John Gilbert and Norma Shearer performing the balcony scene from 'Romeo and Juliet' in the slang of the day. While this film seems virtually unwatchable to today's audiences, it was phenomenally popular in its time, even receiving an Academy Award nomination for Best Picture.

## Rogue Song (1930)

Opera star Lawrence Tibbets, star of the Metropolitan Opera, was signed by MGM to do a movie. A script was developed for him, but when the preview audiences found the rushes to be too serious, MGM went looking for ways to lighten it up. The film was well into production when Laurel & Hardy were borrowed from Hal Roach to portray 'burlesque desperadoes.'

Even though Hal Roach directed the scenes containing Laurel & Hardy, there were still certain constrictions placed upon them by MGM. When shooting was over, they happily went back to what MGM executives called 'that little lot down the street'—the Lot of Fun.

*Rogue Song* is a lost film. Aside from some soundtracks which have been released in album form, only three minutes of the film are known to exist. Luckily for Laurel & Hardy fans, the clip is one of the Boys' scenes, wherein they run into a dark cave together to escape a storm. Ollie's inquiry as to where Stanley got his fur coat is answered by a low, long growl.

MGMP-21400

**Right:** *Stanley and Ollie are oblivious to the knife-wielding lunatic in* The Laurel & Hardy Murder Case.

**Opposite:** *The Boys have knocked down the chimney trying to put up a radio antenna in* Hog Wild.

### Hog Wild (1930)

Despite Ollie's protests that he has a date with Stanley, Mrs Hardy (played by Fay Holderness) insists that Ollie put up the radio aerial. After enlisting Stanley to help him, Ollie calls out, 'Try KFVD!,' the station from which they had just hired T Marvin Hatley.

The house was merely a prop built specifically for this film. Stanley manages to send Ollie from the roof down the ladder and into a garden pond several times. In the script, but not used in the film, was a gag where Ollie gets out of the almost empty pool, looks at the camera, then proceeds to turn on a faucet to fill the pool.

### The Laurel & Hardy Murder Case (1930)

Stanley and Ollie must spend the night in a spooky mansion when they discover that Ebenezer Laurel has died, and that Stanley may be in line for an inheritance. Throughout the night, however, the other heirs are rapidly disappearing. The Boys are frightened by the usual suspects — a black cat, a bat, lightning and a white sheet. A sweet little old lady tries to do away with her fellow heirs, and in her struggle with the Boys, is unmasked as a man (Del Henderson).

At the end, the Boys wake up, and are struggling with each other in a shared dream — yet another Laurel and Hardy film in which the entire story turns out to be a dream.

Filming of **The Laurel & Hardy Murder Case** began shortly after a tragedy in Laurel's life. His wife, Lois, gave birth to a son, Stanley Robert Jefferson — Stan had not yet legally changed his name to Laurel — but the birth was premature and the baby died nine days later. The macabre story and setting of **Murder Case** probably didn't help Stan to recover from his loss, and the film is noticeably devoid of the inventiveness and hilarity customary to a Laurel & Hardy short.

**Right:** *Mr Laurel and Mr Hardy are babysitting their sons, Stan and Babe, in* Brats.

**Below, right:** *Stan and Babe playing chess in* Brats.

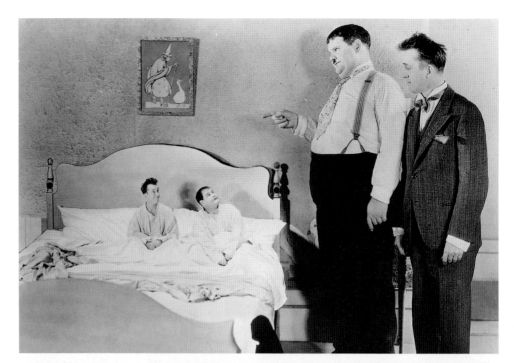

### Brats (1930)

Laurel and Hardy play two fathers, as well as their two sons. In the script they are referred to as Mr Laurel and Stan, and Mr Hardy and Babe (Hardy's nickname) to distinguish between the two generations.

For the split screen shots, the camera was positioned exactly three times as far away, and the sets for the Stan and Babe sequences were built exactly three times scale. The film did not rely upon special effects for its humor, however.

As in **Beau Hunks**, Jean Harlow's photograph appears in this movie, but Jean Harlow doesn't. Unlike **Beau Hunks**, this time the photo is incidental and inexplicable—probably part of an in-joke between friends.

Another interesting side note—this film features the first usage of the Laurel & Hardy theme song, 'Coo Coo.' Written by a 25-year-old musician from Oklahoma named T Marvin Hatley, the song was overheard by Laurel and Hardy in a restaurant and incorporated into their very next film—**Brats**. 'Coo Coo' was originally composed to serve as a time signal at radio station KFVD, played every hour on the hour.

## *Pardon Us* (1931)

Laurel & Hardy's first feature-length film — 56 minutes — ***Pardon Us*** was originally intended to be a two-reeler. The sets, as designed by Frank Durloff, proved to be so elaborate and expensive, however, that Hal Roach decided to make the film a feature, to try to recoup some of the expense. Laurel and Hardy were not enthusiastic about the longer format, knowing the risk of trying to be funny for three times as long a stretch. They had the chore of expanding the script to feature-length.

***Pardon Us***, a burlesque on prison life, contained a big fire scene. Director Jimmy Parrot had prepped the large crew that as a signal to the stagehands to start the fire, he would pull a handkerchief out of his pocket. After everyone was assembled, Parrot, forgetting all about the signal, had to blow his nose, pulled out his hanky, and naturally, the stagehands pulled out the blowtorches. Walter Long, who played 'The Tiger,' a wily convict, was waiting for his cue when suddenly his hair was set on fire. Long lost the hair on the back of his head for no reason: the scene was eventually cut.

**Above: *Bootleggers Laurel and Hardy are getting a lecture on proper respect for authority from the warden in* Pardon Us.**

**Right:** *The new wife in one room and the blackmailing ex-girlfriend in the other—what else can go wrong for poor Ollie in* **Chickens Come Home?**

**Below, right:** *Laurel and Hardy's suspicious wives check up on them as escaped maniac Mae Busch looks on in* **Come Clean.**

## Chickens Come Home (1931)

Mae Busch is a sultry sweetheart from Ollie's youth come to blackmail him now that he is a successful—and married—fertilizer dealer and mayoral candidate. His wife, played by Thelma Todd, comes into the office to pay Ollie a visit and Mae is hidden in a closet. Mae's white fur coat hasn't made it into hiding with her, so Ollie must stuff it up his coat. Inevitably, when Mrs Hardy notices the coat, Ollie must offer it to her as a Christmas present, despite the fact that, as she points out, it is only July.

## Come Clean (1931)

'Mr Hardy holds that a man should always tell his wife the whole truth. Mr Laurel is crazy too.'

The Hardys' quiet, romantic evening at home is disrupted by 'those Laurels.' Mrs Hardy (Gertrude Astor) and Mrs Laurel (Linda Loredo) have every right to be suspicious: the Boys have brought home escaped lunatic Mae Busch.

## *Laughing Gravy* (1931)

'Mr Laurel and Mr Hardy stuck together through thick and thin—one pocketbook between them—always empty.

After discovering that Stanley and Ollie are breaking his rule against dogs, the landlord (Charlie Hall) throws their little dog, Laughing Gravy, out into the snow. Ollie's attempt to rescue Laughing Gravy results in his being locked out in the freezing weather. Meanwhile, Stanley has reeled in the pooch with a knotted bed sheet and is cuddling his pet in the warm bed. When Ollie finally gets back in from the cold, the landlord comes in waving a gun and orders all three of them to leave his boarding house.

After knocking himself out cold and getting soaked with the dog's bath water, the landlord finally gets his wish. Just as Stan, Ollie and Laughing Gravy pack up and are about to leave, a policeman puts a quarantine sign on the door, stipulating that no one can leave the boarding house for two months.

**Above: *The Boys are out on the roof with Laughing Gravy, the dog. If they don't get rid of him, the landlord will evict them.***

**Above: In One Good Turn the Boys are trying to sell their car to help their widowed friend avoid foreclosure. Unfortunately for them, she was only practicing for a play.**

## *One Good Turn* (1931)

When Stanley and Ollie overhear a banker (James Finlayson) threaten to foreclose on a kind old lady (Mary Carr), they rush out to raise the money for her mortgage. Their total assets amount to one 1911 Ford, one 1861 tent, one union suit, two shirts and three socks, but they nevertheless decide to sell their car to pay the old lady's mortgage.

When the Boys discover that the old lady was actually rehearsing a scene for the Community Players and needs the money far less than do Stanley and Ollie, Stanley violently attacks his partner. The script was altered because Lois, Laurel's young daughter, had taken a dislike to Hardy after seeing him bully Laurel time and time again. Laurel changed it to show that Stanley could take care of himself if the situation warranted.

## *Helpmates* (1931)

Believed by many to be the finest Laurel & Hardy comedy ever made, *Helpmates* recounts the attempts of the Boys to clean up Ollie's house after he has 'pulled a wild party.' As the opening titles explain, 'While the cat's away, the mice start looking up phone numbers.' Stanley and Ollie, of course, prove to be less than efficient cleaning partners, eventually burning down the Hardys' house.

The studio built a 'regular five-room bungalow' to be burned down for the final scene. The studio fire department stood by to extinguish the fire when the desired effects were achieved. The effects of the Great Depression were just beginning to be felt at Hal Roach Studios—no longer would five-room houses be built simply to be burned down.

**Above:** *Laurel's efforts to help Hardy clean up after a wild party reduces the house to shambles in* **Helpmates.**

**Above:** *Old Army buddies Laurel and Hardy are knocking on doors, looking for orphaned Miss Smith's grandparents in* **Pack Up Your Troubles.**

## *Pack Up Your Troubles* (1932)

Stanley and Ollie's army buddy, Eddie Smith, has fallen in action, and the Boys assume the care of his motherless child. They set out to find the grandparents of the little moppet (London-born Jacquie Lyn), knowing only that the name is Smith. At a wedding, the Boys prompt the father of the bride to strangle a bridegroom named Smith when they ask him if the little girl is his.

With the discovery of Jacquie Lyn, the script was altered to give her more footage. Hal Roach believed, erroneously, that she would be a star to rival another of his discoveries, Spanky McFarland of the *Our Gang* series.

## *Their First Mistake* (1932)

The battling Hardys separate when Arabella (Mae Busch) leaves Ollie because, as he tells Stan, 'She says that I think more of you than I do of her!'

'Well, you do, don't you?' Stanley asks, but Ollie doesn't want to go into that. Stanley suggests that the Hardys adopt a child to occupy Arabella's time, so she won't mind when Stanley and Ollie go out together.

When they return with the baby, however, Arabella has gone to live with her parents, and the Boys must care for it themselves. The film ends with Stanley and Ollie trying to get the baby and themselves to sleep. The script, however, has the Hardys reconciling. Mae, having struck upon the same idea as Stan, comes home with not one baby, but two.

As so often happened on Laurel and Hardy films, the Boys ad libbed so much on the set that there wasn't time to finish acting the script, so they simply changed the ending.

**Above: *The Boys have brought home a baby for Mrs Hardy. Unfortunately, Mrs Hardy has left for good so it's up to Stanley and Ollie to take care of the little tyke in* Their First Mistake.**

**Above: *Sleepy Stanley is supposed to drive Ollie home from the hospital in Country Hospital.***

## *County Hospital* (1932)

Ollie is enjoying the most peaceful time in his life — he's just beginning a two-month stay in the county hospital — when Stanley comes to visit. After using Ollie's traction weight to crack nuts, Stanley ends up dangling the doctor out the window on the end of Ollie's traction pulley, prompting the doctor (Billy Gilbert) to order them both out of the

hospital at once. Before leaving, however, Stanley sits down on a hypodermic. The nurse who discovers this remarks that Stanley is going to sleep for a month.

Stanley falls half asleep upon starting the engine of his car, and is barely kept from dozing off by repeated taps on the head from Ollie's cast. Narrowly missing cars and trucks, the dozing driver finally smashes up the car so that it is nearly bent double.

**Overleaf: *The hilarious result of Stanley's sleeping and driving— look who's at the wheel now!***

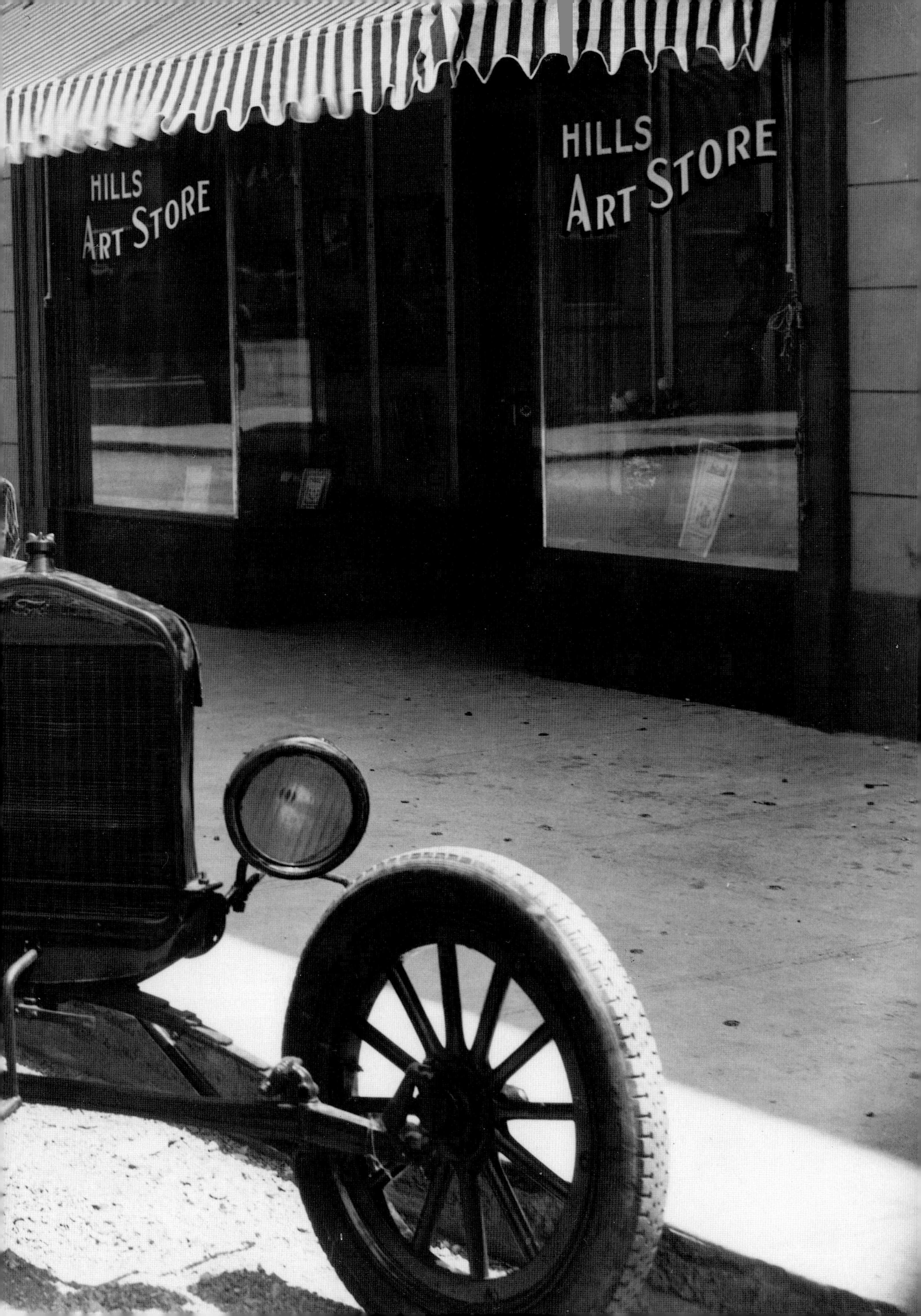
HILLS
ART STORE
HILLS
ART STORE

**Above and opposite:** *The Boys are trying to deliver a piano, through the fountain, over the balcony but never through the unlocked front door in* **The Music Box.**

## *The Music Box* **(1932)**

Possibly the best-remembered Laurel & Hardy film, **The Music Box** is a masterpiece of comedic build-up. The Boys must deliver a player piano to a house—but the house is located at the top of a 131-step staircase. On the way up, they meet a nurse with a baby carriage, a grouchy cop and Professor Theodore von Schwarzenhoffen (Billy Gilbert).

According to Roy Seawright, head of the optical department at Roach Studios, there was a real piano in the crate. 'They needed it to be there for the weight,' he explained.

Stanley walks Ollie right up to the top of the stairs, up a couple more, and right into the garden pool, where the piano joins Ollie in the water.

After mastering the stairs, the Boys attempt to put the piano into the house—through a second-story window rather than the unlocked front door.

48

Above: *In Scram!* vagrants
Laurel and Hardy are having a
drink with the judge's wife, at
least until he gets home.

Opposite, above: *Laurel and
Hardy are tired of selling other
peoples' fish in* Towed in a Hole.

Opposite, below: *At the film's
finale, Ollie only has a bucket to
counter Stanley's hose, so he
resorts to persuasion to convince
Stanley not to drench him again.*

## Scram! (1932)

A hard-nosed judge (Rychard Cramer) orders vagrants Stanley and
Ollie to leave town. When they plead not guilty, the judge asks, 'On
what grounds?' Stanley replies, 'We weren't on the grounds. We were
sleeping on a park bench.'

Upon leaving the court house, the Boys encounter a dapper drunk
who, in gratitude for their help in finding his car keys, invites them to
spend the night at his house. When they arrive, however, he can't seem
to find his house keys. Stanley and Ollie clamber in through a window.
The drunk man tells them to make themselves at home, then leaves
when he realizes that he is at the wrong house.

Nattily attired in their unknown host's pajamas, the Boys meet the
lady of the house (Vivian Oakland), who faints. The water they use to
revive her turns out to be gin. After her second glass of the 'water,' she
dissolves into laughter. Amicably, the Boys join in. Upon this cozy scene
enters the man of the house, the judge.

### Towed in a Hole (1933)

Fishmongers Stanley and Ollie agree upon Stan's million-dollar idea:
'If we caught our own fish, we wouldn't have to pay for it. Then whoever
we sold it to, it would be clear profit.' Impressed, Ollie says to Stan, 'Tell
me that again.' 'Well,' says Stan, 'if- -if you caught a fish and whoever
you sold it to, they wouldn't have to pay for it—then the—profits would
go to the fish.' He tries again. 'If—er—if you—.' He gives up and blows
his horn.

The two trundle off to the junkyard to find themselves a fishing boat.
They must fill it with water to test its seafaring capability, and of course,
Ollie is soaked a dozen different ways by Stan. The skirmish escalates
until Stanley is left armed with the ultimate water fight weapon—a
hose. Ollie, clearly outmatched, convinces Stanley that they are both
far too mature to throw water at each other.

**Above: *In* The Devil's Brother, *the Boys are in over their heads with the bandit Fra Diavolo's schemes.***

## The Devil's Brother (1933) (Fra Diavolo)

Based on the 1830 comic opera *Fra Diavolo* by Daniel F Auber, **The Devil's Brother** is set in eighteenth-century Italy. The Boys play Stanlio and Ollio, characters based on Auber's Giacomo and Beppo. Stanlio and Ollio are given a choice of servitude or death by the evil Diavolo (Dennis King), who has disguised himself as the Marquis de San Marco. Stanlio and Ollio choose servitude, though they have not mastered the use of the sedan chair. In front of the townspeople, they drop their new master on the ground.

Hal Roach was hoping that this 90-minute film would establish Laurel & Hardy as feature-film stars and himself as a full-length-movies producer. The reviews were mixed, except in France, where Hal Roach recalled, 'I saw the picture in France, and when every song came on, the whole damn audience joined in.'

## Me and My Pal (1933)

Successful businessman Ollie is slated to marry the daughter of oil magnate Peter Cucumber in the afternoon. In the morning, his best man, Stan, arrives with his wedding present. While waiting for the taxi to take them to the church, Ollie opens up the present—a jigsaw puzzle. The two become engrossed in putting together the pieces. Soon, the taxi driver, the policeman, Ollie's butler and the telegram delivery boy are all participating as the hour of Ollie's wedding comes and goes.

The original title, **The Best Man**, was changed to make a play on the name of the latest Spencer Tracy movie, **Me and My Gal**.

HR-L13-7

**Above: Me and My Pal are too busy putting together a crossword puzzle to go to Hardy's wedding, along with the butler, taxi driver, policeman and telegram delivery boy.**

**Left: The Boys are cleaning chimneys in Dirty Work. Too bad the chimney didn't survive the experience.**

## Dirty Work (1933)

Chimney sweeps Stanley and Ollie go to work at the home of Professor Noodle. The professor is working on a youth rejuvenation formula, which transmogrifies a duck into an egg. When Ollie accidentally falls into the tank, he emerges regressed into a monkey wearing a derby.

**Right: *Stanley and Ollie check the cellar for a prowler in* The Midnight Patrol.**

**Opposite: *In* Busy Bodies, *Stanley is carefully putting up a nail for Ollie's jacket, but no one has noticed the water spurting from the wall—yet.***

### The Midnight Patrol (1933)

Officers Laurel & Hardy investigate a call about a prowler breaking into a house. After many efforts to get inside the house themselves, they get their man—only it's Chief Brassbottom, who had locked himself out.

One funny scene which was deleted from the film has Stanley telling Ollie a riddle which he has made up: 'What is it that people eat, covered with skin and filled with meat, and whistles like a skylark soft and sweet?'

Ollie, puzzled, looks at his sandwich and asks, 'Whistles like a skylark?' Stanley nods affirmatively.

Stanley asks, 'Do you give up?'

Ollie, seeming a little ashamed, answers, 'Yes.'

Stanley triumphantly supplies the answer to the riddle: 'A hot dog!'

Ollie indignantly replies, 'A hot dog doesn't whistle like a skylark!'

'I know it doesn't. I just said that to make it hard.'

### Busy Bodies (1933)

Stanley and Ollie are working at a sawmill where they spend most of their time cleaning up their own messes. Stanley pounds a nail into the wall as a coat hook, not realizing that it's going through the water pipe on the other side.

***Busy Bodies*** has virtually no plot—the short is really more of an excuse to string together a series of gags. Without the responsibilities of propelling a plot and introducing a lot of side characters, the Boys were free to do what they did best—creating a lot of havoc in a simple situation.

**Above:** *Mrs Hardy is spoiling Hardy while he tries to convince her he needs to take an ocean voyage. Then, while he and Laurel are at the Sons of the Desert convention in Chicago (opposite), the ship goes down.*

## Sons of the Desert (1933)

The Sons of the Desert, the fraternal lodge to which the Boys belong, is having its annual convention in Chicago this year, and the Boys have taken a solemn oath to attend—without having consulted their wives.

Ollie, after chastising Stanley for not being the king of his castle, tries to convince his wife (Mae Busch) that he has had a nervous breakdown and must go on an ocean voyage—which will actually be his trip to Chicago. She prepares a tub of hot water for Ollie's feet. After Stanley knocks both her and himself into it, Mrs Hardy throws the tub at Stanley but misses, and it crashes over Ollie's head.

This film was in the works for two months before filming began, in an effort to avoid the patchiness that marred previous feature productions *Pack Up Your Troubles* (1932) and *Pardon Us* (1931). The reviews were excellent, and the film was a hit at the box office. Many comedy teams had difficulty making the transition from two reelers to feature length films, but critics and audiences alike were pleased to find that the comedy was 'funny all the way through,' and 'without the benefit of the usual distressing formulae of padding and stretching.' (Andre Sennwald of the *New York Times*). *Sons of the Desert* was among the 10 top-grossing films of 1934.

Twenty members of the American Legion were among the sixty extras employed as fellow Sons. The fan club 'that goes beyond a simple fan club' took their name from the title of this film. When Stan Laurel heard about the genesis of Sons of the Desert, he told them, 'The only thing I really insist on is that everybody have a hell of a lot of fun.'

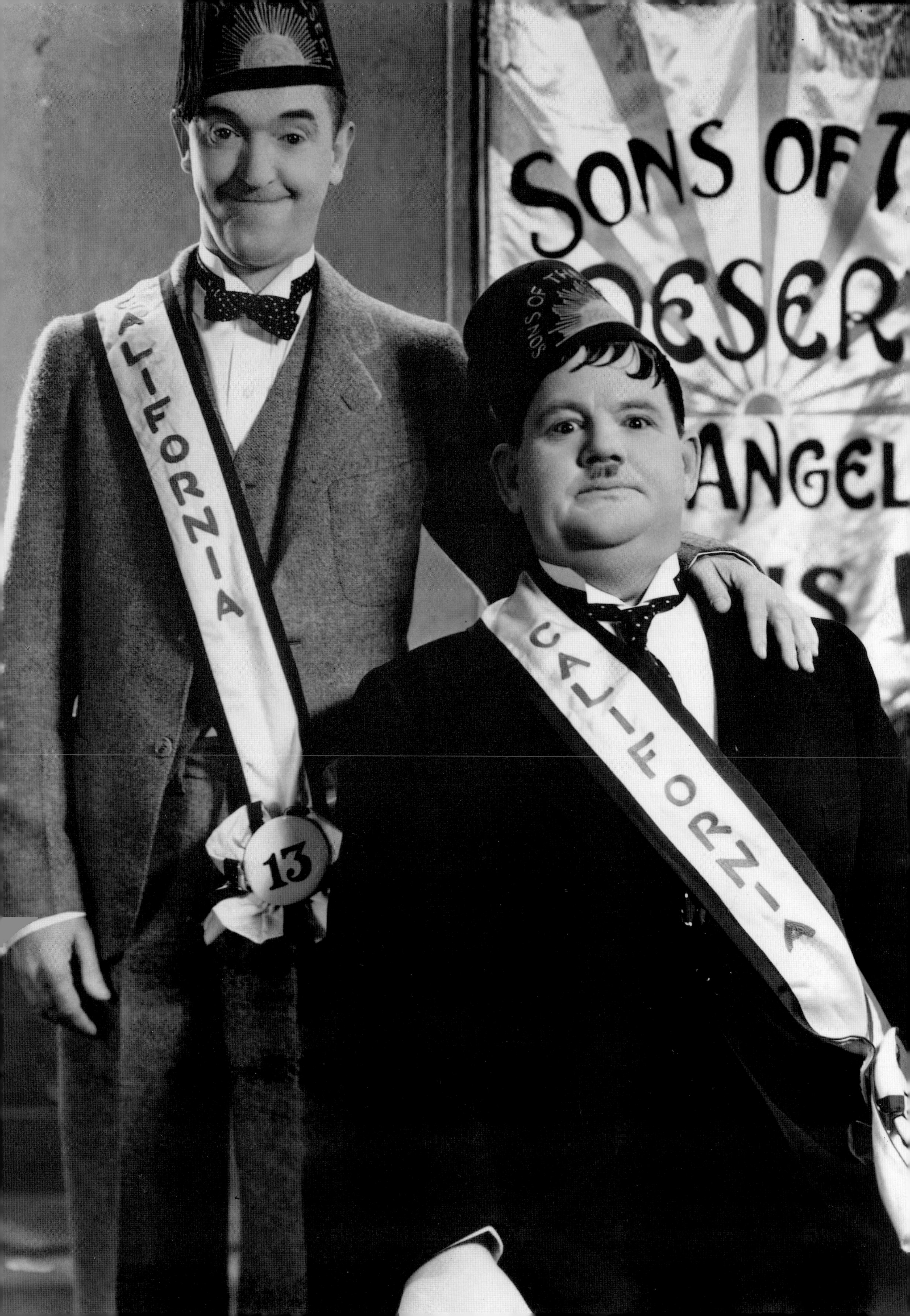
SONS OF
ANGEL
CALIFORNIA
13
CALIFORNIA

**Above:** *Laurel and Hardy are star witnesses at killer Walter Long's trial, and think they're putting him away for good in Going Bye Bye.*

**Right:** *Long has nearly escaped and the Boys are knocked down and caught in the crush as the crowd flees the courtroom.*

**Opposite:** *This scene from Going Bye Bye never would actually appear in the finished film.*

## *Going Bye Bye* (1934)

The Boys have brought state's evidence against a notorious criminal, Butch Long, who swears revenge against Stanley and Ollie. As the guards take him off to serve his term of life imprisonment spewing vitriolic threats, he nearly breaks loose, causing the courtroom spectators to stampede, trampling over Stanley and Ollie in their panic.

The Boys decide to leave town, and advertise for a traveling partner to share expenses. Unfortunately, they find Butch's moll (Mae Busch), who is helping the escaped criminal to get out of town. The scene shown in the still *opposite* did not actually take place in the film, but amply illustrates the plot machinations.

**Above:** *The well water has been spiked with a bootlegger's liquor, but the Boys and Mae Busch don't know it in* **Them Thar Hills.**

## Them Thar Hills (1934)

Ollie is gouty and must go to the country for a rest. 'Drink plenty of water—and lots of it!' the doctor instructs him. Meanwhile, in the mountains, bootleggers who are trying to evade federal agents dump their moonshine into a well.

Moments later, Stanley and Ollie arrive at the house they've decided to rent in the mountains and are elated to find the well. 'It's just what the doctor ordered!' Ollie exclaims.

Stanley is struck by the color and taste of the water, but Ollie assures him that there is simply iron in it. 'It tickles,' Stanley replies.

They begin to sing 'The Old Spinning Wheel' when a knock comes at the door. Mae Busch and her husband, Charlie Hall, have run out of gas and want to borrow some fuel. Mae is thirsty and is served some of the well water. While her husband takes the fuel to their car, Mae waits with the Boys and has some more of the delicious water. The high spirits of

the threesome upon his return leads Charlie to the wrong conclusion: 'What do you mean by getting my wife drunk?' he demands, and the ensuing fight involves feathers, molasses, a plumber's helper, butter, kerosene and a fateful match.

**Above: *Mae Busch's husband has all fingers pointing at him this time in* Tit for Tat, *the sequel to* Them Thar Hills.**

## *Tit for Tat* (1934)

Stanley and Ollie are entrepreneurs opening up a new electrical supplies store. All friendly relations with their next door neighbor, grocer Charlie Hall, are destroyed when Charlie realizes that this duo are the same fellows who got his wife (Mae Busch) drunk in a mountain cabin, then cut off a lock of his hair and glued it to his chin as a beard. Policeman James C Morton tries to keep the situation equable.

*Tit for Tat* is the only Laurel & Hardy sequel—the follow-up to *Them Thar Hills* (1934). The short was nominated by the Academy of Motion Picture Arts and Sciences for Best Live-Action Short Subject.

## Babes in Toyland (1934)

Laurel & Hardy play Stannie Dum and Ollie Dee, two apprentice toymakers who are fighting to save Mrs Peep (Marie Wilson) from getting evicted from her home, a large shoe, by evil Silas Barnaby (Henry Brandon), who has the mortgage papers. Barnaby is in love with Little Bo Peep, played by Charlotte Henry, and will tear up the mortgage papers if Bo will give him her hand in marriage. To save her from his clammy clutches, Stannie Dum dresses up as a bride, pretending to be Bo, until he can get the mortgage torn up and Bo safely married to her true love, Tom-Tom (Felix Knight).

When the Boys have to venture into Bogeyland, however, Barnaby sics the Bogeymen after him. Two of them chase the Boys into the toy factory, where Stannie Dum and Ollie Dee pelt them with darts and eventually save the day.

Hal Roach bought **Babes in Toyland** from Victor Herbert for Laurel & Hardy. The only problem was that there was no plot. On his train trip home to Los Angeles from New York, Roach was determined to write a story. Laurel, however, had many reservations, including a dislike for feature-length films. Their disagreement over this film was the beginning of the end of the Lot of Fun.

**Above: *Stannie Dum and Ollie Dee fight the Bogeymen in Babes in Toyland.***

**Opposite: *Stannie and Ollie pose with Little Bo Peep (Charlotte Henry) in a publicity still from Babes in Toyland.***

## Bonnie Scotland (1935)

This movie went through several different incarnations, first as **Kilts**, then **Laurel and Hardy of India**, then **McLaurel and McHardy**. Then one day during production, Laurel left Hal Roach Studios, claiming he had been fired. The official studio explanation was that they were unable to come to an agreement with Laurel on story ideas. The studio claimed in an article in *Variety* that Hardy would remain at Roach and begin another series called **The Hardy Family**, costarring Patsy Kelly and Spanky McFarland.

Stan told the press that the rescinding of his contract was a complete surprise. There had been difficulties working on the story, but they had all been settled. He said, 'I was amazed when I was notified the picture had been called off and my contract terminated.'

A reporter found Oliver Hardy on the golf course that day and asked him about the split up of his comedy team. 'We've not broken up. We're the best of friends. He and I have been together longer than seven years and our team must not be broken up.'

On 27 March 1935, when Laurel and Hardy walked into the Cocoanut Grove arm in arm, resplendent in dinner jackets and broad grins, it became obvious to the press and the studio that the pair was definitely still a team. Hardy had rejected the chance to have his own series out of loyalty to Laurel. The united front of their two most famous comedians caused the studio to negotiate another contract with Stan, but the rift caused on the set during the making of **Babes in Toyland** would have future impact on Laurel & Hardy.

## Our Relations (1936)

The Boys have received a letter from Ollie's mother, telling them that she found a photograph of their twin brothers who ran off to sea, joined a mutiny and were hanged. Rumors of their deaths are greatly exaggerated, however, and sailors Bert Hardy and Alfie Laurel cause much confusion when their ship docks at the little seaside town that is the home of Ollie and Stan. The plot revolves around these mistaken identities, involving harbor doxies, suspicious wives and the town gossip. The plot thickens as gangsters arrive looking for Bert and Alfie, but instead find poor Stanley and Ollie.

**Above: *Laurel and Hardy are making Swiss cheese in front of Charles Juddels in Swiss Miss.***

## *Swiss Miss* (1938)

Mousetrap salesmen Stanley and Ollie decide to sell their traps down at the cheese factory, where they figure there will be need for them. Stanley makes Swiss cheese out of Emil's (Charles Juddels) samples to help promote the mousetrap business, while an approving Ollie looks on. (This gag was never used in the film.) The Boys proceed to drill holes in the floors so that the mice have a way to get into the factory.

Stan Laurel's problems with Hal Roach came to a head on this film. One of the most memorable sequences in filmed comedy, where Stanley and Ollie carry a piano across a rickety bridge, was altered without Laurel's knowledge. Roach decided to delete a previous scene, in which a devious chef plants a bomb in the piano. The bomb will be triggered when a certain key is hit. Once the bomb footage was edited out, Stan's drunken stumblings against the piano have lost all their suspense. Laurel was furious when he discovered the alteration.

## Saps at Sea (1940)

After 13 years of partnership, Stan Laurel and Oliver Hardy fool around together on the set. This was the last film they made for Hal Roach Studios. Roach, a shrewd businessman, had kept Laurel and Hardy under separate contracts which never came up for renewal at the same time. In 1939, Stan decided that he would never sign another contract without his partner, whose contract would not end until a few months later.

In the interim, Laurel and Hardy made **The Flying Deuces** (1939) for an independent producer. That same year, Hardy made a forgettable film, **Zenobia**, costarring comedian Harry Langdon. Laurel was busily tidying up his personal life and polishing material for use in his post-Roach era films. He anticipated that he was just about to come into the height of his powers as a comic and a film maker.

When Hardy's contract expired several months later, they negotiated a deal with Twentieth Century-Fox. Stan's dreams of artistic freedom and creative control of his films were not to be realized, however. Fox had little understanding of Laurel & Hardy's humor, and used them as buffoons in mediocre love stories. The team chose to fulfil their contracts without complaint or protest, as though they deserved this fate for having left Hal Roach in the first place.

# THE TWENTIETH CENTURY-FOX YEARS

**S**tan Laurel was always loyal and supportive—often financially—of his old friends, Ben Shipman among them. Shipman was the attorney for Stan Laurel Productions, but he was a shy and retiring lawyer who had never purposefully gotten involved with show business. He didn't have the shrewd street-fighting instincts necessary to make a deal with a major studio like Twentieth Century-Fox. Consequently, the Boys' new contract would make them wish they had never left the Lot of Fun.

Twentieth Century-Fox had no understanding of the sweet and innocent nature of Laurel & Hardy comedy that endeared the duo to their fans. The scripts produced at Twentieth Century-Fox refer to the Boys as 'a rather sorry-looking pair of dopes,' 'jerks,' 'half-wits,' and other contemptuous names; they portray the Boys as mean-spirited wise-acres, whose function is merely to provide comic relief to mediocre love stories. The sympathy of the audience is directed to the 'normal' characters who have to put up with Stanley and Ollie's stupidity, which is exactly the opposite of the philosophy at Roach's studios. The Fox scripts pit Stan and Ollie against each other, thereby eliminating the friendship that had been the heart of their comedy. The Fox films feature slick production values and shabby one-liners, and lack the warmth, gentleness and humanity of the Roach films.

To make the situation completely hopeless, their contract and the structure of a huge studio gave them even less control over their pictures than they'd had at Roach's. Fox even made the Boys alter their appearance so that they looked more like normal people—their clothes fit better, and they no longer wore the very light make-up that had given them such an other-worldly aspect in their earlier films.

Stan and Oliver were upset and ashamed by the pictures they were making and the treatment they received, but they didn't complain. Some of the people who were working on the set have said that Stan and Oliver would have had more control if they had complained to the

front office about their bad directors and miserable scripts, but the Boys were far too stoic and polite.

In 1942, Hal Roach was drafted into the army as a lieutenant colonel, and the Roach studios began producing training and propaganda films. The Lot of Fun as Stan and Oliver had known it was now just a memory.

Instead they went to MGM, which was not known for having an adept touch with visual or broad comedy. MGM was successful with comedies that featured sophisticated, witty dialogue like **The Thin Man** series, but had practically ruined the careers of the Marx Brothers and Buster Keaton because the studio did not allow them any creative control. Unfortunately, the same held true for Laurel & Hardy's movies.

Stan was mortified by the eight films that Laurel & Hardy completed after leaving the Roach studios. 'What was there for us but to get out?' he asked. 'We had done too many films in our own way for us to keep taking anything like that, so we gave up the ghost. It was sickening.'

Instead, the Boys embarked on an enjoyable music hall tour of England, Ireland and Scotland, performing a sketch written by Stan. They were among the most popular personalities on television in the early 1950s, which was extremely gratifying to them, though they weren't receiving any residuals because the old shorts were owned by Hal Roach. Both Oliver and Stan finally found themselves in stable marriages. Oliver remained happily married to Lucille Jones Hardy from 1940 until his death in 1957, and Stan's marriage to Russian concert singer Ida Kitaeva Raphael lasted 20 years, until Stan's death.

**Previous page and opposite: In 1941, after an ill-fated move from Hal Roach Studios to Twentieth Century-Fox, Laurel and Hardy optimistically joined MGM for two films, Air Raid Wardens and Jitterbugs (both 1943). Unfortunately, they still hadn't found the creative freedom and support they were looking for.**

**'The writers never bothered with us,' said Hardy in a 1951 interview. 'Our producer never read our scripts. "You boys don't need a story," he'd tell us. "Your pictures are making money; what more do you want?"'**

**Stan added, 'Naturally, it breaks your heart.'**

**Above: A classic Mr Laurel and Mr Hardy pose.**

## A-Haunting We Will Go (1942)

In their second film for Twentieth Century-Fox, the Boys get involved with the Mafia, who hire them to transport what they believe to be a corpse. The cargo turns out to be a live fugitive from the law, Darby Mason. With the unintentional assistance of con men, a magician named Dante and the Boys, Mason is safely delivered into the arms of the law.

## Jitterbugs (1943)

As proof of how little Fox studios understood Laurel & Hardy's comedy, the Boys appeared in **Jitterbugs** as 'zoot-suited swing musicians,' forcing Laurel to deliver lines such as, 'Come on, hep cats, we're going to spread a load of jam!'

Fortunately, part way through the film, the Boys disguise themselves as Aunt Emily (Stan) and Colonel Bixby (Oliver), who prove irresistible to the gold-digging Lee Patrick.

## The Dancing Masters (1943)

Ollie steps on some toes when the Boys play dance instructors who must help a young inventor to impress his girlfriend's father. The plot is garbled, but at least some old Laurel & Hardy skits are tossed in. They don't make too much sense out of context, however, and critics mistakenly put the blame for this poor film on the shoulders of Laurel & Hardy.

Opposite: *Another fine mess in* A-Haunting We Will Go.

At top: *The Boys posing for* Jitterbugs.

Above: *A still from* The Dancing Masters. *Neither Laurel nor Hardy look too pleased about this film.*

**Above and opposite:** *Laurel and Hardy's last film,* Atoll K. *Sadly, the Boys were finally beginning to show their age.*

## *Atoll K* (1951)

The last film to feature Laurel & Hardy, this confused production was an agonizing experience for anyone who wrote, directed, acted in or saw this disaster. To produce the script, the French government, who were funding this film, ensconced four writers in a luxury hotel outside of Paris and told them to collaborate. Unfortunately, the two Americans, one Frenchman and an Italian had very little in common in the way of language, so they decided to write separate scripts. Four very different scripts with disparate approaches to the story were the end result, and attempts to assimilate into one cohesive whole failed miserably.

When Stan Laurel finally got to read the story, he said to the writers with a crack in his voice, 'Is this what you did all these months, boys? Did you really expect us to accept this rubbish?' Writer Frederick Kohner left Paris immediately, knowing that the script was terrible.

The language barrier continued on the set, and the script girl was the only person in the entire crew who understood French, Italian and English. All of the actors delivered their lines in their native languages, so there was very little chance of any ad-libbing. Because *Atoll K* was

filmed out of sequence, it was next to impossible for Laurel to add his own ideas to the script.

To compound their problems, there was a debilitating heat wave which caused Hardy's health to deteriorate rapidly. He developed an irregular heartbeat, while Laurel, experiencing painful prostate trouble, became far too thin, his weight dropping from 165 to 114 pounds.

Originally scheduled to last 12 weeks, filming continued for 12 months, but Laurel and Hardy stayed because they felt obligated to complete the film. When production finally wrapped in April 1951, Laurel and Hardy returned to California and tried to recover their health.

**Atoll K** was released in France and Italy that November, and in England as **Robinson Crusoeland** the following year. It went unreleased in the United States until 1954, when a small distributor, aptly named Exploitation Productions, tried to capitalize on the Laurel & Hardy name, releasing the film as **Utopia**. It is a testament to the chaotic nature of this production that no one had remembered to copyright the film in the United States, so, ironically, this calamity is by far the most easily available of all the films this team made together.

# THROUGH THICK AND THIN

### *This is Your Life*

One evening in December 1954, Stan Laurel and Oliver Hardy were honored on the television show ***This is Your Life***. Their first outing on the smaller screen, it was to be their last appearance together. Both had been suffering various illnesses just prior to this unrehearsed—indeed, unannounced—television debut. Host Ralph Edwards had to ad-lib uncomfortably on live television for several minutes after the NBC cameras surprised Stan and Oliver at New York's Knickerbocker Hotel. The excuse given was that it took longer than anticipated for Oliver to walk from there to the El Capitan Theatre where the show was filmed, but Stan's later criticism of the show has prompted speculation that the comedians were late because Stan had to be persuaded to go through with the show.

The lake on the Hal Roach Studio lot was renamed Lake Laurel and Hardy with a plaque which reads: 'So named because these two world famous comedians were first teamed here at the Hal Roach Studios, and because they, more than any others, were in and out of these waters.' Hal Roach, Sr and his son, Hal Roach, Jr, were on hand for the ceremonies.

In 1955, Stan and Ollie made a deal with Hal Roach, Jr, for whom both had a great deal of affection, to do a television series. ***Laurel and Hardy's Fabulous Fables*** was to have been a series of one-hour shows in color, written by Stan. Unfortunately, the series was never made, due to Stan's failing health.

Increasingly concerned about his own health, Oliver went on a diet. He lost 150 pounds, bringing his weight to 210, lower than it had ever been in his adult life. At Stan's suggestion, the pair had some new publicity photos taken—Ollie hardly looks like himself.

Early in the morning of 14 September 1956, Oliver Hardy suffered a massive stroke, paralyzing him and leaving him unable to speak. He was moved by the hundreds of encouraging letters he received. Less than a year later, he went into a coma, and on 7 August 1957, he died.

Oliver was a man of many interests. It was said that his skill as a golfer made it almost unnecessary to hold the annual Hal Roach tournament because the outcome was almost a foregone conclusion.

LAKE LAUREL AND HARDY

SO NAMED
BECAUSE THESE TWO
WORLD FAMOUS COMEDIANS
WERE FIRST TEAMED HERE AT
THE HAL ROACH STUDIOS
AND BECAUSE THEY
MORE THAN ANY OTHERS,
WERE IN AND OUT OF
THESE WATERS

"THIS IS YOUR LIFE"
DECEMBER 1, 1954

There was a weekly poker game in the Hardy home, and he loved horse racing, even buying a stable in his later years. He was an excellent cook, and his singing voice won him applause whenever he could be persuaded to perform. He loved to hunt deer and quail, until one day when, at the age of 45, he shot a deer and saw its dying expression. He never hunted again, nor did he or his wife eat the animals he raised on his farm.

Oliver's personal life, like Stan's, was plagued by gossipmongers, who sensationalized his several marriages. In his third marriage, to script clerk Virginia Lucille Jones, Oliver seemed to find real happiness until his death at age 65.

Oliver probably would have liked his obituary in the *London Times*: 'He was tall as well as fat, and he had a handicap of 10.'

After Oliver's death, Stan kept his promise that he would never perform without the partner who had been loyal to him in the face of studio pressures. In 1960, Stan received a Special Academy Award 'for his creative pioneering in the field of cinema comedy.' Stan continued to write comedy until he died of a heart attack on 23 February 1965.

Stan was a gracious and generous man. During World War II, he threw lavish dinner parties for sailors and soldiers. His closest friends throughout his life were from his vaudeville days, and he arranged for many of them to get work or even helped support them financially. He had spent most of his time working, contributing to all aspects of his films, especially directing and writing. He always considered himself more of a writer than a performer. Stan had been a man of few hobbies—he fished a little, and dabbled in gardening, once cross-germinating a potato and an onion. His daughter, Lois, recalled that he couldn't get anyone to eat the resulting vegetable.

Stan had a great respect for his fans, and in his retirement, he entertained the people who rang his doorbell wanting to meet him. Stan answered all of his fan letters personally, and even kept his name in the phone book. He continued to write comedy and often sent his ideas to friends.

Stan greatly enjoyed the work of Jackie Gleason, Art Carney, Lucille Ball and Jack Benny. When he saw his own films on television, he wanted to re-edit them to eliminate the long silences which had once accommodated the laughter of a theatre audience. 'On television, the films seem so slow,' he lamented. 'Sometimes you think they'll never end.'

Only three things could cause Stan to lose his good temper in his later years: poor editing of his films for television, the sensational articles about his five marriages and alleged poverty, and the memory of the shameful treatment he'd received at the hands of Twentieth Century-Fox in the 1940s.

Stan mellowed a great deal with age, but he remained a practical joker throughout his life. One day in a stationery store, the clerk seemed to recognize him: 'Say, aren't you—' and Stan replied, 'Oliver Hardy.' 'Right,' exclaimed the clerk. 'Whatever happened to Laurel?' Stan replied sadly, 'He went balmy!'

Part of the enjoyment in watching Laurel & Hardy shorts is seeing the warm and loving friendship between two fine comedians who remained loyal to each other in Hollywood, a world as full of pitfalls and villains as the short films Laurel & Hardy produced there. Though the villains sometimes seemed to come out on top, Laurel and Hardy triumphed in maintaining their gentle dignity and humor, and creating two of the most beloved characters in the history of film.

# FILMOGRAPHY

*Lucky Dog* (1919)*
*Forty-Five Minutes from Hollywood* (1926)*
*Duck Soup* (1927)
*Slipping Wives* (1927)*
*Love 'Em and Weep* (1927)*
*Why Girls Love Sailors* (1927)*
*With Love and Hisses* (1927)*
*Sailors Beware* (1927)
*Do Detectives Think?* (1927)
*Flying Elephants* (1927)
*Sugar Daddies* (1927)
*The Second Hundred Years* (1927)
*Call of the Cuckoo* (1927)
*Hats Off* (1927)
*Putting Pants on Philip* (1927)
*The Battle of the Century* (1927)
*Leave 'Em Laughing* (1928)
*The Finishing Touch* (1928)
*From Soup to Nuts* (1928)
*You're Darn Tootin'* (1928)
*Their Purple Moment* (1928)
*Should Married Men Go Home?* (1928)
*Early to Bed* (1928)
*Two Tars* (1928)
*Habeas Corpus* (1928)
*We Faw Down* (1928)
*Liberty* (1929)
*A Perfect Day* (1929)
*They Go Boom* (1929)
*Big Business* (1929)
*Wrong Again* (1929)
*Berth Marks* (1929)
*Double Whoopee* (1929)
*That's My Wife* (1929)
*Men O' War* (1929)
*The Bacon Grabbers* (1929)
*Angora Love* (1929)
*Unaccustomed As We Are* (1929)
*Hollywood Review of 1929* (1929)

*The Hoosegow* (1929)
*Nightowls* (1930)
*Blotto* (1930)
*Rogue Song* (1930)
*Hog Wild* (1930)
*The Laurel & Hardy Murder Case* (1930)
*Be Big* (1930)
*Brats* (1930)
*Below Zero* (1930)
*Another Fine Mess* (1930)
*Our Wife* (1931)
*Pardon Us* (1931)
*Chickens Come Home* (1931)
*Laughing Gravy* (1931)
*Come Clean* (1931)
*One Good Turn* (1931)
*Beau Hunks* (1931)
*Helpmates* (1931)
*Any Old Port* (1931)
*Pack Up Your Troubles* (1932)
*Their First Mistake* (1932)
*County Hospital* (1932)
*The Music Box* (1932)
*Scram!* (1932)
*The Chimp* (1932)
*Towed in a Hole* (1933)
*Twice Two* (1933)
*The Devil's Brother* (1933)
*Me and My Pal* (1933)
*Dirty Work* (1933)
*The Midnight Patrol* (1933)
*Busy Bodies* (1933)
*Sons of the Desert* (1934)
*The Private Life of Oliver the Eighth* (1934)
*Hollywood Party* (1934)
*Going Bye Bye* (1934)
*Them Thar Hills* (1934)
*Babes in Toyland* (1934)
*The Live Ghost* (1934)

**Above: *Although Rogue Song was directed by Lionel Barrymore, their frequent director, James Parrot, appears in this photo between Stan and Oliver, along with opera star Lawrence Tibbets.***

*Tit for Tat* (1934)
*The Fixer Uppers* (1935)
*Thicker Than Water* (1935)
*Bonnie Scotland* (1935)
*The Bohemian Girl* (1936)
*Our Relations* (1936)
*Way Out West* (1937)
*Pick a Star* (1937)
*Swiss Miss* (1938)
*Blockheads* (1938)
*The Flying Deuces* (1939)

*A Chump at Oxford* (1940)
*Saps at Sea* (1940)
*Great Guns* (1941)
*A-Haunting We Will Go* (1942)
*Air Raid Wardens* (1943)
*Jitterbugs* (1943)
*The Dancing Masters* (1943)
*The Big Noise* (1944)
*Nothing But Trouble* (1944)
*The Bullfighters* (1945)
*Atoll K* (1951)**

*Stan Laurel and Oliver Hardy both appeared in these films,
however, they were not yet the team of Laurel & Hardy.

**Also released as *Robinson Crusoeland* in 1952 and *Utopia* in 1954.

# Index